How to Prepare a Sermon

Simple Steps to Super Sermons

Bill Taylor

Foreword

I have known Bill Taylor for more than 50 years. We first met when he was Youth and Music Director at Forest Hill Baptist Church in Jackson and I was but a mere youth in his youth group. We were both just getting started in the ministry. While our paths diverged over the years, we did occasionally see each other, so I have been able to keep up with his ministry to some degree.

Bill mentions that his educational pursuits were "limited" to college studies. I beg to differ. I would suggest that while that may be true of his formal education, his educational pursuits have included much more. His learning has included a lot of practical experience in the "ordinary" world of a bi-vocational preacher and pastor. From that perspective, he has learned much, and what he has learned comes through clearly in this book.

There are at least two ways to learn to preach. One is to get formal training. The other is to get experience. The problem with formal training is that you must also add the experience for the training to become effective. Bill comes at us from the perspective of experience. In this book he shows us the value of practical learning in the basics of communicating the biblical message to the church. He has practiced what he is preaching here.

Bill makes clear his purpose in this teaching manual. He wants to help those who are beginning like he did (and I did) more than 50 years ago. While our paths have gone in different directions and I have spent the last 30 years seeking to train preachers from the biblical perspective in several different venues at New Orleans Baptist Seminary, Bill has been practicing his gifts. However, one thing I have learned from my formal education and my teaching experience is that probably the most efficient way to reach people is for their peers to speak to them from a common experience. Bill is a peer to those he seeks to help. I commend him for this effort and pray God's blessings on the results of his labors.

Starting with the basics, Bill proceeds to help the student learn what is involved in preaching and how to prepare for it from the original desire to preach to the delivery of the sermon. I especially appreciate the good words about the importance of the text and context in preaching and his good advice that expository preaching--simply exposing the Scriptures--is the best route for a preacher of any kind to follow.

This work is filled with wisdom that comes from the experience that produced it. Here is an example from Chapter 5:

You are not ready to begin sermon preparation until you understand, as fully as possible, the meaning of the text. Ask first what it meant to the writer and those who first heard it. Next ask how the text has been understood through the history of the church. Finally, ask what the text means to you personally and finally what should this text say to those who hear your sermon on this text.

You are not prepared to answer any of these questions until you grasp the meaning of the text in your own mind. Look away from the printed words and try to recall the full statement of the text. It would be great if you could memorize the text, but many people cannot quickly memorize new verses. You can achieve a fairly complete textual knowledge

*by reading and re-reading the text. It is also helpful to read
the same words from several translations. The goal is to be
able to fix the text in your mind.*

*After the text is fixed in your mind, begin choosing the study
aids you will use. This can be the most critical step you make.
Unless you understand the text on which you base your
sermon, there is a high probability you will not preach a
biblically sound message.*

In addition to the good and wise advice on the text and the
context, Bill also gives some important information on some
resources for sermon preparation. His listing and description
of resources in printed books, ebooks, software, and online
resources is excellent and well presented.

I commend this work especially to preachers and others who
are starting out without the benefit of formal training. Even
those of us who have benefited from "education" might find
some good help here also.

Jim Dukes
Senior Professor of Greek and New Testament
Director of Prison Programs
New Orleans Baptist Theological Seminary
Orlando, Florida

Contents

PREFACE

Who can preach? This is a practical, but not technical approach to the task of preparing sermons. I only offer a few basic skills which any beginner can employ, and a skilled preacher may only find minimally helpful. Those who have little formal ministerial education will probably benefit the most, or at least find it helpful. Those who have preached for years and have earned advanced degrees may not find it as fruitful. If you are a fortunate person who already knows everything I have written here; please pass it along to someone who has not had the same privileges as you.

My formal education was limited to college studies. My further education has come from 55 years of persistent personal study of the craft and gifts of preaching. Preparing a sermon is a daunting task for many of God's servants who have not had formal training and even to some who have seminary degrees. I have one friend who left the ministry as a pastor because he said he simply could not prepare enough sermons to fill the church's needs. He is a good godly man who earned both college and seminary degrees. Preaching a sermon, which is fresh and helpful to your congregation, is a difficult task when you consider you will need to repeat the task about three times each week, more than 150 times each year. To fill this role requires creativeness, craftiness, thoughtfulness, giftedness and many other talents which must be surrendered to hearing and saying only what God wants you to say. It is daunting. I am overawed when I read that some of the great preachers actually preached every day. Whew!

This is an important question ... "who is permitted to preach?"

In the New Testament it seems that almost everyone could preach. The act of preaching is simply telling forth the truth about Jesus. Our primary source of subjects and information for preaching is the Bible, which is God's Holy Word. Preaching which is void of Bible truth is not Christian preaching.

Preachers perform an essential and important duty for the church. Some are not officially the pastor of a church. One of the first recorded sermons in the history of the church is found in the Bible. It is recorded in Acts chapter 7 verses 1 through 53. The sermon was so powerful, its logic so irrefutable, that the angry leaders of the Jews, put the preacher to death by stoning, right on the spot. His name was Stephen and his official title was not preacher or pastor ... he was a deacon. He was also the first martyr of the Christian church. Preaching is not a safe business to enter.

At times, preaching is seen as a glamorous occupation in American society. However, preachers and preaching are always subject to attack by the enemies of God. Who knows, the time may come swiftly in America, when preachers will be scorned and disenfranchised by society at large, or by a government attempting to quieten dissidents. One thing is increasingly apparent ... the Bible is not held in high regard by the courts and legislators of The United States of America.

If you are determined to be a preacher, one who is true to God and His word, you may find yourself under the same type of attack, which the judge who recently posted the Ten Commandments, recently endured. Be confident that, like the

Ten Commandments, God will preserve you through the fiery trials of civil rebukes. The Apostle Paul warned that "*All who live godly lives in Christ Jesus will suffer persecution.*" We should wonder why we are not being persecuted for preaching in America. Most of what we preach is in direct opposition to the tides of our times.

If you think by learning to preach, that you will be earning yourself some earthly accolades, then you are beginning from the wrong perspective.

I believe, from personal experience, and from the evidence of Scripture, that God calls certain men to be His preachers. The Old Testament prophets are excellent examples of this fact. The prophets came from varied backgrounds and most resisted God's promptings to be prophets. Some were rough and outgoing, others were scholarly and refined. The gospel accounts of the New Testament, tell the story of Jesus calling His disciples one by one. Each had a personal call, and each had a specific ministry to fulfill. And each accepted Jesus' call as a lifetime commitment. Tradition tells us that all fulfilled that calling to the end, with the lone exception of Judas.

Some of the best preachers I ever heard were not licensed or ordained by any denomination. The great Keswick preacher, Ian W. Thomas, is a prime example. But most of the great preachers I have heard, have gained the approval of a respected local body of elder believers. If God called you to preach, I advise you to seek the approval of a Bible believing Christian church. The accountability they will require of you will benefit you and your ministry. Your acceptance by qualified men will help open doors for your ministry. There will be times when you need the help of men more experienced than yourself. It is more difficult to get help from qualified men if you wait until you are having difficulties, than it is to gain their respect and support in the beginning of your ministry.

In the New Testament, preachers were required to receive the approval of the local church they attended. It they could not pass the scrutiny of those who knew them well, it was feared they may not faithfully proclaim the truth when they were no longer under the supervision of the elders of their church. The same principal is still valid.

The Bible lists the characteristics and requirements for those who would be pastor-preachers in I Timothy 3:1-7, *Whoever aspires to be an overseer desires a noble task. [2] Now the overseer is to be above reproach, faithful to his wife, temperate, self-controlled, respectable, hospitable, able to teach, [3] not given to drunkenness, not violent but gentle, not quarrelsome, not a lover of money. [4] He must manage his own family well and see that his children obey him, and he must do so in a manner worthy of full[a] respect. [5] (If anyone does not know how to manage his own family, how can he take care of God's church?) [6] He must not be a recent convert, or he may become conceited and fall under the same judgment as the devil. [7] He must also have a good reputation with outsiders, so that he will not fall into disgrace and into the devil's trap. NIV.*

Then, who can preach? The answer is anyone whom God has chosen to bear reproach for the name of Jesus. Do not begin, unless you are willing to bear persecution for doing so.

Our physical bodies possess natural processes which attempt to reject transplanted organs. Since new believers are inserted into the body of Christ, which is the church, the church body will either accept or reject them. Every believer needs to be accountable to, and live agreeably with, other believers. There should be no 'lone wolf' mentality among God's preachers. The natural desire for Disciples of Christ is to bring people to Jesus and plant them in a fertile field of believers where they will grow up and become ardent disciples of Jesus. Jesus said, "he *who does not gather with Me, scatters.*" Luke 11:23

Each denomination has its own set of guidelines and requirements for those who are permitted to be the preachers or pastors of their churches.

The denomination's requirements may be very simple, or highly complicated. Some require a full seminary education in order to regularly stand in the pulpits of their churches. I am not qualified to argue with any denomination about their requirements. However, if you wish to preach in a particular denomination, you should quickly seek to meet their standard requirements.

Other denominations only require "evidence" that God has "called" this man to preach and that his beliefs are in line with others in his denomination. Some regulate the pastorate through a presbytery, conference or board; others rely upon the entire local church body to make autonomous decisions about who is permitted to preach.

If I meet a man who has gained the full approval of his denomination, and his denomination is known to be biblically sound, I will more readily embrace his ministry and I believe more people will be open to hearing his message.

The simple truth about "non-denominational" preachers is that many of them could not gain the approval of a wise council of elder believers. The reasons for their rejection may be bad doctrine or bad behavior. These men have difficulty gaining traction in their ministry. Stay with your church, or become a member of a church which believes and practices the truth of the Scripture; then seek their approval upon your ministry. We should all desire to cooperate with others who believe in our Lord Jesus Christ.

I am a Baptist minister. I have always served Southern Baptist churches as a pastor, preacher, teacher, musician and youth leader. In my group of Baptists, local churches appoint an Ordination Council to examine candidates who express a desire to preach. The Ordination Council either approves or disapproves the qualifications of the candidate. The next step toward becoming a pastor is to gain the approval of a local church which asks the man to become its pastor. These simple requirements are often regarded by some other denominations as flawed and too easy. The system works as well for Baptists as other systems of other denomination.

Most young Baptist preachers serve small churches, or work on the staff of larger churches as a form of apprenticeship and on the job training. In my ministry I have done both. As a teenage boy, I 'led the singing' for two separate churches at separate times. These were unpaid positions and I did not consider myself as being "in the ministry." My first "job" in the ministry was to serve a church as a combination youth and music minister. I served this church for about a year and a half. Then I began preaching for a small congregation in a country church after one year. During the year and a half I was on the staff of Forest Hill Baptist Church, in Jackson,

MS, I spoke to youth gatherings and other groups in order to gain experience.

While one denomination may approve of a man too quickly, another may reject a man too quickly. In either case it is a sad mistake. It seems obvious, that there needs to be some procedure which reliably approves or disapproves of a candidate for the ministry. Whatever the requirements are, you should comply with them, just as you must meet entry requirements to enroll in a school.

In the brief epistle of 2nd John, verses 8-9 lay down further requirements which the Apostle of Love gave to an early church where he had been their pastor. *"Look to yourselves, that we do not lose those things we worked for, but that we may receive a full reward. Whoever transgresses and does not abide in the doctrine of Christ does not have God. He who abides in the doctrine of Christ has both the Father and the Son."* John knew that the wrong preacher could lead his *"little children"* astray, and he wanted no part of that.

Regardless of your denominational requirements, you should seek to gain as wide a background of study as possible. The first requirement is that we show ourselves to be *"approved unto God"* but since we must minister to men, we need the approval of godly men as well.

I did not have the opportunity to attend seminary in my studies for the ministry. In some denominations, that empty spot on my resume would disqualify me for the ministry. I have never used the lack of formal education as an excuse for mediocrity. I encourage you to not slip into the role of one, who because of his own lack of opportunity, rails against those who have had the privilege to receive the finest education. The simple, obvious truth is: there are qualifications other than mere education which qualify you to be a "man of God." My old friend and mentor, Dr B. Philip Martin, used an expression which has often encouraged me to continue to pursue excellence in knowledge and ability. Here's what he said: "God can use a dull axe or a sharp one, but the sharp axe makes a smoother cut, and can therefore be used in places a dull blade could not."

I admire men who have had the opportunity to receive formal education in college and seminary. I also admire men who, though they did not have advanced ministerial training have nevertheless conscientiously continued to learn and grow as ministers of the gospel. A man of humility will quickly admit that he needs all the help he can get. The challenge of *"rightly handling the word of truth"* is too great for any mortal man to accomplish with nothing but his native ability. We need, and should seek and rely on the aid of God's Holy Spirit; as well as getting the help of other gifted men of God.

You may live where no teacher is available. I urge you to take advantage of the many sources of Christian training that are available. Many fine colleges, universities and seminaries provide training opportunities for preachers and other ministers. Be careful to avoid the snare of a 'diploma mill.' The certificate they sell you signifies to any learned person that you are nothing but a poor person who was duped into thinking he has been educated when in fact he has been deceived.

Seek out reputable schools, highly recognized authors who have gained the confidence of men from more than one denomination. Purchase your books from stores that refuse to sell the books of cults, fakers and phonies. Build a good library of books by faithful men whose works is accepted by trustworthy men.

This book will attempt to help a preacher with limited skills do sermon preparation and build a sermon, which is biblically sound, and helpful to his hearers. If this book is helpful, you should not stop with this basic effort. Use it only as a first step, continue to find other books which lead to further growth and development of your preaching skills.

I am only attempting to cover some bare necessities. If it gives some struggling preacher a kick-start, I will have accomplished my goal. There are hundreds of scholarly books which have been written on this subject by men far more qualified than me. I yield to their abilities, yet continue to write. This book is written for men like me who want to preach their very best, but yet have not had the opportunity to develop their skills to a point they would like to reach.

There is no substitute for making a lifelong study on the subject of how to preach. I have several books on preaching in my library and have gained immensely from each of them. My father, who was a Baptist Preacher from a previous century, recommended I buy a book by Dr John A. Broadus, "A Treatise on the Preparation and Delivery of Sermons." Reading that book was my first effort to begin to understand the art, craft and skills of preparing and delivering a sermon. It is a great book that guided many of my early efforts in learning to preach. Books and tools are helpful if we seek the faithful guidance of God's Holy Spirit. As you study, God will make you aware of your deficiencies and show you how to become the preacher God called you to be. It does not appear to be God's method, to call equipped servants. It seems, rather, that God equips each servant He calls to serve in His kingdom.

When I began my college education I chose to major in public speaking, otherwise described as a "Speech Major." I learned of a great many tools which have served me well over the years, but you do not learn to preach or prepare sermons in a class for public speaking. A public speaker learns to speak upon any subject under the sun. A preacher must get his subject material from a limited source, the Bible. A preacher must focus all his abilities in public speaking to the goal of making God's truth so plain that even a child could not err after hearing him speak. A preacher should not desire to be thought of as a dynamic or entertaining speaker. God's preacher must desire above all, to please God with what he says and how he says it.

Preaching is not unique to Christian churches, but the subject and content of Christian preaching differs from any other form of public speaking. Other forms of speaking, such as philosophy, may focus upon presentation of such powerful evidence, that the hearer is overcome with intense logic or rhetoric. Christian preachers also present powerful arguments, but we do so with no thought of overwhelming the hearer with our abilities. Once we have finished our speaking, and in fact, before, during and while we are preaching, we rely on the powerful presence of God's Holy Spirit to convince, convict and convert the hearer about the truth.

Dr Bill Bright, founder of Campus Crusade for Christ, taught more Christians to present the gospel in a one-on-one format than perhaps any other man who has lived. He gave this profound definition to bearing personal witness to Jesus.

"Witnessing is: sharing the gospel with another person, and leaving the results up to The Holy Spirit." When a preacher stands before a congregation, he can do no more than an individual speaking to another individual. We share the truth of God, and leave the results to The Holy Spirit. To use a paraphrase of Dr. Bright's formula: "Preaching is sharing the gospel with a person or group of people, and leaving the results up to The Holy Spirit."

Other forms of public speaking are justifiably focused on entertainment of an audience. In their trade, emotionally engaging the hearer is not a trick or gimmick; it is a necessary element to keep the attention of the hearer. But the preacher cannot let his sermon deteriorate into a purely entertaining device full of tricks and gimmicks. We rely on the drama in which our listener's life is embroiled to produce the effect of keeping the hearer involved emotionally.

Part One

THE SERMON

What Is A Sermon?

The first step of preaching is to realize the differences between public speaking and preaching.

The actual presentation of a sermon is similar in manner to public speaking. Jesus' sermons were often part of a conversation He held with His audience. His listeners often asked Him questions and He responded with answers which were fascinating, and held all the appropriate spiritual truth. When He was asked a legal or political question, He answered it in such a way that it not only contained the legal or political answer, but also presented the truth of God on the subject.

Preaching is far more difficult than public speaking. Public speaking only has to please the audience of people. Preaching is directed to the audience, but is adjudicated by the unseen, ever present God. We are unable to see a change in God's expression when we get off course and begin to chase rabbits, rather than hunt the varmint.

Like public speaking, a sermon may employ many different forms. The function of a sermon may entertain, instruct, explain or inspire, but it is void until it contains a pure, direct call to action, which is based on and confirmed by God's Holy Word. We are not just interested in passing out information, we intend for men to be confronted by the truth of God while being exhorted and encouraged to make an appropriate response.

A Sermon is Foolishness

That is not my choice of words; those are the Apostle Paul's words used to describe what God called us to do. "*The message of the cross is foolishness to those who are perishing, but to us who are being saved it is the power of God.*" 1 Corinthians 1:18. The reason people have not already responded to the gospel message is that they think it is foolish to do so. It is your primary job, with the full assistance of the Holy Spirit, to convince men to trust in Christ's provision for their sin on Calvary's cross.

To whom is preaching foolish? It is not foolish to God. It is not foolish to those who have heard the gospel, believed its truth, repented of their sins and received the fullness of God's Holy Spirit to dwell in their life. God is the one who appoints and anoints preachers to carry the gospel to the four corners of the globe. God causes their '*foolish*' preaching to be fruitful to the salvation of a billion souls. Preaching is not foolish to God. He delights to reveal the false wisdom of the world in its true character. He makes the wisdom of this world appear, as it is ... foolish. He is thrilled to use unworthy men like you and me to do a service, which holy angels would be delighted to do.

Preaching is only foolish to those who are perishing. Those who are perishing, rail against the preacher. They are like a drowning man who curses the lifeguard who throws him a lifeline. They try to drown the swimmer who is trying to lead them to safety. Even those who know they need to hear, still resist with all their might.

Do not imagine you will be thought of as one of the world's wisest men just because you are a preacher. It would be better for you to think of yourself as a *"fool for Christ's sake."* I'm not trying to discourage any man whom God has touched and turned his heart to the lost and dying men of Adam's race. Nor would I discourage you if your ministry seemed only to help those who had already come to saving knowledge of the Lord Jesus.

However, I do want to forewarn you that the road you are embarking on is a long and difficult one. The least difficult object you will encounter is learning to prepare and deliver a sermon. The more difficult tasks are keeping your way straight and keeping your own sinful passions and foolish impulses under control. If you are easily discouraged, you are no different from those who have gone before you. We all stumble and fall, we all are forced repeatedly to fall on our knees before a Holy God and beg for mercy, forgiveness and strength to carry on.

And when our strength is renewed ... we once again turn to face the burning fire of the world's heated resistance, and seek to quench the flames with a simple message about God's Son who came and died upon a cross for our sins. It is a certain fact, that if we had to accomplish this in our own strength, we would become a victim of the flames we are trying to quell. Thank God, we are not alone in this struggle. God not only has called you to preach, He has pledged to help you in your struggle to become the best preacher you can be, and He will sustain you against the bitter attacks of our common foes, the world, the flesh and the devil.

As long as we are in this world, there will be those moments when under the withering attacks of Satan, we question the wisdom of doing, what God in His wisdom called us to do. I am sure that when we finally stand before Him in the presence of His holy angels, we will finally realize we were not fools at all. We will know with eternal certainty, while greeting our friends around the throne, that we held in our bosom and delivered with passion the message that is the power of God for salvation.

A Sermon Has A Plan

A sermon outline is a man-made plan, or diagram for spoken communication. The purpose of an outline is to aid the preacher in organizing his thoughts, which in turn helps the listener to follow his progress through his sermon. When a man leaves his outline, his listeners will say 'He's chasing rabbits." This old expression came about when dogs that were trained to hunt game would leave the pursuit of a fox, to chase a rabbit. Keep your focus on your subject and try your best to present your thoughts in an orderly fashion. If your outline does not make sense to you, it probably will not lead your audience to the proper conclusions. Outlines can be very basic and only list the main points of the message. Sermon outlines may be much more complex and list sub headings under the main thoughts. If you need to extend an outline further you may list subheadings underneath subheadings.

Many preachers find it wise to complete each thought in the outline. When I first began to preach I often used outlines that could be written on one side of a 3 x 5 note card. The outline consisted of a title, a text and three or four main thoughts and ended with a suggested appeal appropriate to the subject. At that time, this was adequate as I had time to think thoroughly about what I would say under each main point and I was only preaching one new sermon each week.

A lot of time has passed since I first began to preach and I still have a few of those note cards in a box. As I look at them occasionally I have several impressions. First, I had a very poor style of printing. Next, I have no idea what I said after the main points. Finally, if I needed to use the outline again, I would have to completely rebuild the sermon. This does not pose a problem at all as I preach a new sermon almost every time I approach the pulpit.

If God graces your life and gives you a lengthy ministry, you may need to re-use some of the messages you prepare. The outlines will be absolutely useless at a future time, unless you flesh them out to the point that another person will have an 'almost complete' understanding of the subject which you had outlined.

When an unskilled person draws a plan for a building, he may be the only one who understands how the pieces fit together to build a complete structure. When a trained, skilled architect draws a building plan ... any knowledgeable contractor can follow his plan and complete the building, often without even speaking to the architect. We should make it our goal to design our sermon plan in a manner that anyone could use it. If we accomplish that, we will be able to re-use it after time has erased our original thought process.

A Sermon Is Proclamation

The basic definition for the word "preaching" had in the original manuscripts the meaning of "telling forth." In the Old Testament, the prophet was given a message directly from God. The messages were received under very different circumstances and were delivered in a wide variety of methods. No matter which method of delivery the prophet used to deliver his message, when he did so, he was "telling forth" the message he had received from God. Prophets often began their proclamation with the phrase, "The Word of The Lord."

Speaking for God is the factor which makes preaching diametrically different from other forms of public speaking. When we stand before people to preach we should be "telling forth" the "Word of the Lord." This is no time to get cute, or invent a fanciful thought; this is the moment for which God placed His hand upon your life and moved you to become His preacher.

A Sermon makes a point

The introduction portion of a message is usually the point in a preacher's message at which he is the most inventive. You may use almost any tool to gain attention and bring the minds of your audience to focus on the subject you intend to preach.

When speakers from other venues stand to speak, they may mention many different unrelated subjects. Preaching seldom follows that pattern. When people listen to a sermon they should not be forced to ask: 'what's the point?'

Our message must be clear. The listener must know what you had to say, if not from the very beginning, at least by the time you have finished. This is the point the Apostle Paul was

making when he said: "*If the trumpet gives an uncertain sound, who will prepare for battle?*"
I Corinthians 14:8.

Our point, or points, must be based on scriptural truth and all points should carry you in the direction to your concluding point. It is imperative that our message is in agreement with the word of God. If the message is not in line with the word of God, we are not speaking the truth. Everything we say must be in complete agreement with God's word.

A Sermon makes a plea

Your skills as a preacher will be tested by two basic criteria. First: Is the message in agreement with God's word? Second: Does the message help the hearers apply the truth to their life? Most listeners quickly forget the exact phrasing of our sentences, but will remember a truth which they can easily apply to their daily life.

We must present the truth in practical ways, so that our hearers can 'live out' what they learned. Jesus did this with words, which even unbelievers remember and quote.

He often quoted a familiar scripture passage, then gave it its proper interpretation His interpretation was often different from the one given it by His unbelieving critics. "*You have heard that it was said, 'An eye for an eye and a tooth for a tooth. But I tell you not to resist an evil person. But whoever slaps you on your right cheek, turn the other to him also.*"
Matthew 6:38-39. The Jewish teachers of the law were giving interpretations to scripture that were false. Their ideas and interpretations marred, blurred and scarred the true image of

God. Jesus spoke to correct their error and plainly stated the truth of God.

The understanding of scripture by unbelievers, and some believers, is often deficient and usually not accurate. Preachers are to be the truth tellers who correct the inaccuracies about God which are being told in our generation. Jesus called the false teachers of the law *"blind guides",* who caused their followers to fall into a ditch. The importance of preaching the truth, the whole truth and nothing but the truth cannot be overemphasized. The struggle to know the truth without error is an endless task.

Part Two

WHAT MOTIVATES PREACHERS?

1

The Preacher's Motive

e first step in preaching is to clearly understand the motive for preaching, which is separate from motives from the other forms of public speaking.

There is a basic motivation which applies to all the preaching we do. You should know why you have surrendered to God's call to preach. This is your motivation and will be your guiding star when times of doubt and discouragement come.

As a young man, I came to understand that God wanted me to preach. How I understood this is difficult to explain. I resisted what I describe as my "Call to Preach." I didn't want to be a preacher. Over a period of time as I prayed, studied God's word and sat under some very good biblical preaching, I finally surrendered my life to obey God's will.

The time I spent struggling and resisting God's call upon my life was a very difficult and emotionally troubling period of time which came to an immediate end, when I surrendered to God's will. My uncertainty ended and I knew a peace and purpose which is impossible to describe. I had feared the act of preaching and the rigid lifestyle that would be required. But after surrendering to God's will, I immediately embraced every aspect of the life I was entering. Exhilarating excitement replaced doubt and fear. I pray that you have had a similar, though very different, experience before choosing to be a preacher.

I did not notice at first, but over time a sense of urgency grew inside me, which at times I felt physically. Old Testament prophets described that feeling as "*fire in his bones.*" Mine feels more like a fire in my belly. The message God gives me is like a hot coal from which I must deliver myself. After more than 55 years of preaching, I still have a fire inside me, which urges me to prepare new sermons and present them wherever God provides an audience. I have never refused an opportunity to preach and have seldom preached the same sermon to a congregation on more than one occasion. God always gives me something to say that is new and fresh.

What motivates you to preach? Every Christian is a potential preacher. Anyone can be 'called to preach.' God's word charges all believers to be willing and ready to preach at any moment. "*Be instant in season and out of season.*"

I can say, based on many experiences, that if we are called upon to preach without preparation, or forewarning, we will be gifted miraculously by the Holy Spirit. When God provides an opportunity, He will not fail to provide the words to speak. That principle also applies to the weekly sermon planning of a pastor. We use the talents and skills God has gifted to us, but we must rely completely upon His Spirit to lead us through the process of planning, preparing and preaching a sermon.

Once you have entered this process with the Lord as your guide, you will always look eagerly to another opportunity to sit down with Him and plan another sermon.

Education, experience, talent and tools cannot replace or supplement a lack of motivation. You are responsible to God, to yourself and to your calling to stay motivated. We stay motivated by keeping our devotional life in order and guarding against sin from entering our life and finding a hearty welcome. There is a quaint old saying, "You can't stop the birds from flying over your head, but you can prevent them from building nests in your hair." That needs no explanation, but it means you will make mistakes. Even though you make mistakes you should not welcome them as constant companions on your road of life. Remove yourself from bad influences. Refuse to be in the audience of false teachers. Do not make commitments to causes that do not honor the precious name of Jesus. There needs to be a daily, conscious re-committing to our sacred task of being God's messengers.

Regardless of what seems to discourage you ... you must press on. Every preacher has moments of despair, doubt and questions his motives. Use those moments to revisit why you began to preach in the first place. Renew you commitment to the Lord's plan for your life and ask for His power to help win the battle you are fighting.

Christ's preachers have an unfair advantage

We are in the Lord's business because we love the Lord more than life itself. We do not have to be concerned about our business going out of business. Our commitment includes being willing to go anywhere, do anything and ignore any naysayers standing in our path. Many teachers have successful careers who are completely bored with their subject. No one is exempt from feeling that life is pointless. You can't avoid moments which lack motivation by changing professions. On the other side, many people perform mundane tasks, but they keep their emotions involved, because of an interest in their subject and a sincere desire to share their knowledge or skills.

We too love our subject, but our subject also loves us. He is our dearest friend. He gave His life to redeem us from our sin and to give us an abundant life. Every day He fills our hearts with joy and brings light into dark places into which we stumble. We see lives transformed as we passionately share our wonderfully simple message. When we stand and speak the truth of God's word, we sometimes feel we are superhuman beings, standing on a mountaintop, hurling sanctified spears at mystical powers. The very wonder of the simple words we speak, empowered by the anointing of God, reaching into the minds, emotions and spirits of men we barely know, that work the wonder of God's grace in them ... wow! Who could become bored while doing such a miraculous task?

God speaks of you and your profession. He says: "*He makes His messengers to be flames of fire.*" When we preach, we ignite fires of change and release streams of redemption that spread like fiery floods, that purify and make whole rather than damage or destroy. We have an unfair advantage over all the men who do only the work of man. We are privileged to do the work of God. What a wonder!

We receive motivation from several sources

- Each of us has an innate level of fervor which stems from our human nature. It's just the way we are. We did nothing to acquire our natural temperament, and it may be very different from any of our family members. Some emotions are easily too stirred, while others require a mixer as powerful as a cement truck.
- As we preach, we are aware of the need of our hearers. Jesus experienced this. He said of those who came to hear Him, "*They are like sheep without a shepherd.*" Nothing is more helpless than a sheep separated from its shepherd. God has anointed us be part of this work, "*The Son of Man is come to seek and to save that which is lost.*"
- We are legitimately motivated when we look upon our congregation in a similar manner which Jesus looked upon His. People need the Lord, and it is our privilege to direct their lives to Him.
- It is exciting to speak for God. I believe every member of the body of Christ functions as the eyes, ears, hands and lips of the Lord. Preachers have received a special "unction" to speak for Him. It is an awesome responsibility and an honor, of which no man is worthy. We are aware of the dignity which is conferred upon a man who is named an Ambassador of the Unites States. I would rather have my post than any which a worldly government can confer. I am Christ's Ambassador to the World. I have good news to bring from a God who graciously gives gifts and honestly collects debts.
- Our greatest source of motivation is God's Holy Spirit. I would not want this job without Him. He is a constant comfort, a faithful guide, an empowering presence.

Our audience is always secondary

A preacher must make his hearer secondary to the Lord for whom he speaks. We must speak for Him while we are speaking to men. In the gospels you can read incidents where men tried to distract Jesus from His appointed tasks. While He was always polite to the distractors, He maintained His focus on His primary goal. In this regard, the preacher should never:

- Preach for personal gain;
- Preach for personal fame,
- Preach his personal ideas in lieu of speaking God's message...

2

What is Your Point?

This is the point at which you decide the focus of your sermon. Great sermons use all their smaller points to reach a final conclusion.

There's an old Chinese proverb which states "The journey of a thousand miles begins with the first step." In preaching, the first step is to decide where this message is intended to go. You can't make your point if you don't have one. All preachers have been guilty of trying to preach when they had no certain destination.

As a young preacher, I would place my sermons in certain categories which needed regular attention. I used two major categories and subdivided each one into many sub-categories. The first major category, Evangelistic Messages, had the deliberate intent to share the gospel with unbelievers. The second category, Discipleship Messages, had the aim of helping believers grow in their faith. My plan made the focus of a message aim directly to either lost men, or to saved men.

I preach what I call devotional sermons in Wednesday night prayer services. Devotional sermons are well suited for people who are focusing their life toward a time of prayer. We all need the encouragement of devotional messages.

In my Sunday preaching, I follow a pattern of preaching through books of the Bible, or portions of Scripture. This is a general road map, but I often deviate from this pattern to preach a series of messages on a certain topic or theme such as missions, stewardship, or family life or any other theme, which is needed.

In preaching through lengthy passages of Scripture, I encounter texts that require me to preach on subjects I might have ignored, if I had used any other scheme of preaching. When I encounter such a subject, I have commented that I have never preached that text in a previous sermon. I often get comment from these sermons, to the effect that a hearer had never heard a sermon on the subject and was particularly helped by it. These comments encourage me to believe that we need to preach all of the books of the Bible.

It is my firm conviction that expository preaching through the books of the Bible, or of major bible themes, meets more needs than any other plan we can devise.

Determine your text, then the theme of your text

As early as possible, determine the text on which you will preach, and then determine the main focus of your text. This can be difficult or easy, and I don't know a method that insures it will always be easy. Here are some steps you can use.

- Read the text several times. Read it in various versions. If you have an Amplified Bible, make that one of your reads. If you have a Companion Bible, or study Bible, read all the notes and references it gives.
- Read commentaries which explain the meaning of phrases and words in the text.
- Try to place it in a general category such as evangelistic, doctrinal, informative, historical, worship, or other categories in which you have some background.
- Isolate parts of speech and see if they suggest a pattern. Look first at the verbs, then the nouns, then repetitive phrases or words.
- Is there a word in your text which appears in very few places in the rest of scripture?

Ask questions about the text. I will introduce you to a website in a later chapter of this book which helps students learn the Bible study method called Inductive Bible Study, and which teaches and utilizes this method to perfection.

If your topic cannot be adequately covered in a single message, perhaps you should consider a series. A good series of sermons carefully follows a course of study from start to finish, in similar fashion to an individual sermon. Try to flesh out a general outline for an entire series before beginning on the first message. This will help you prevent being repetitive.

What about texts that suggest several topics?

Sometimes there are several worthwhile objectives in a text or passage. You are obliged to divide the text into multiple messages or preach it as one unit. Preaching such texts as a unit with one primary emphasis is often the best choice. God had a clear intent when He placed all these thoughts in what we may see as a tangled pile. As you study the sermons of other preachers, you will notice that some preachers who are very good at handling large passages of scripture. Follow their example. It may seem they only 'hit the high points.' They are actually tying many twigs together into one bundle. "The Pulpit Commentary" is an old work that covers almost every text in the Bible and offers sermon suggestions on most texts. You can seldom use one of the outlines verbatim because of the old English terms they use, but they are highly suggestive of courses you may follow.

If you choose to preach the entire passage in a single message, use care to surround the central thought of the text with related topics found in the passage. Let the main thought control your message. Be sure lesser points do not disagree with the central theme of the passage. In such texts, you should always look intently for the scarlet thread which connects this text to the Cross of Christ. It is rare for such difficult or rich passages to completely ignore the message of redemption.

3

Choose a Text

Every sermon should begin with the choice of a text. If you veer from this course, you will soon be looking for texts that support your ideas. This may seem too simplistic, but as you preach to the same congregation over time, you will experience great difficulty in choosing a text.

Good sermons always begin with, and are based on a text or texts. There are times that a particular subject becomes appealing and the preacher wants to preach on that topic. There's nothing wrong or abnormal about that thought process. However, you should exercise care when preaching topical sermons, as it is easy for them to stray from a firm scriptural interpretation and spout your own ideas rather than the truth of God.

If you become aware that members of your congregation are involved in pornography, or gambling or some other harmful or dangerous behavior, you would be derelict in your duty if you did not address topics which deal with known needs. But even here, you should begin with a text. A topical Bible is the tool to use to find the right text in these cases. Be sure that the text directs your thinking. Do not try to make the text say what you want it to say.

Be careful about only preaching topical sermons. It is very easy for topical preaching to degenerate from preaching into public speaking. Every topical sermon must have a scriptural basis ... this means they should have a text, which states your basic idea as clearly stated in the Holy Scripture. We are in the pulpit to speak for God. He chose us to preach, but we are not authorized to put words into His mouth. He has instead promised to put the words in our mouth ... words which are backed by solid textual references.

If your idea is not biblical, it doesn't deserve a place in a sermon. To say the same thing in similar words ... If it ain't in the Bible, forget it.

Respect your text

Be careful to avoid misuse of texts. There are verses which have a clear meaning, but have nevertheless been widely misused. One such example is the phrase "Search the Scriptures" found in John 5:39. When that phrase is used as if it were a command, it is being taken completely out of context. I have heard sermons preached on that text, which scalded the hides of believers who did not engage in deep bible study. The verse is not a command to search the scriptures, but it is often quoted and used as if that was the intent of the verse. *"You search the Scriptures, for in them you think you have eternal life; and these are they which testify of Me."*

This is the proper interpretation of that verse: We are not saved by searching the scriptures; we are saved by accepting the testimony of scriptures about Jesus.

The first purpose of Bible study is to understand what a given text means. We must understand what it meant to those who first heard it and what it means to believers who are hearing it today. Then, and only then, we are privileged to construct a sermon plan that makes the message of Scripture clear to our hearers.

God's thoughts are not your thoughts

Don't try to make a text fit your thoughts. There have been times when I opened my Oxford Dictionary to try to determine the meaning of a verse. Words in Scripture are often used differently from their everyday use. Bible scholars have highly technical tools which they use to determine the meaning of words.

Hermeneutics - is a scholar's device which he uses in attempts to bring the true meaning of a specific, single word from one language into the language you speak. Hermeneutics is a study of the principles for sound systematic interpretation of Scripture. I am not a scholar in hermeneutics, so I rely on the scholars who are highly skilled in this area.

Exegesis - is similar to hermeneutics, but is broadly concerned with the meaning of a word considering it meaning within the context. Exegesis attempts to interpret the intended meaning of a text through word meanings, grammar and the context.

To attempt to use these tools without a solid foundation in their function is beyond the skill set of most preachers. Men who devote their lives to scholarly pursuits serve the entire body of Christ by recording and revealing their findings. Many of these men are teachers in denominational seminaries and Bible colleges. Most pastors and preachers rely on the work of respected scholars to resolve the difficult issues and questions about word meanings.

On the level of a preacher who is only "street smart", we are familiar with how a word changes in meaning from one context into another. To a plumber, a joint is the connection of two pieces of pipe with threaded connectors. To a drug addict, a joint is a Marijuana cigarette rolled in cigarette papers. When I was a child, low-class drinking establishments were also called joints. It makes a lot of difference to the hearer, which "joint" you are talking about. The Apostle Paul uses an entirely different meaning when in Romans 8: 17 he says "*we are joint heirs with Christ Jesus.*" Understanding context and actual meaning of words by their use in that context may help you avoid many blunders.

God chose to reveal Himself through the words of men who were in many respects, just like you and me. Each man wrote from the vernacular, the common speech of his time, and from his own experience, his words had specific meanings in his time and locale. God has chosen to use us in a very similar manner today. Unlike the men whom God used to write the Bible, we are prone to say the wrong thing. They wrote, perhaps not knowing the eternal significance of the words they penned. In spite of their personal deficiencies, they miraculously wrote the exact words which God would have them use. It is my prayer, that as I preach, I will use the exact words which God wants me to use, so I might convey the meaning of His word to the people who hear me preach. I'm sure you will pray a similar prayer about your preaching.

Simple methods for choosing texts

The most common way in which a sermon text is chosen is while reading the Bible. A text seems to literally jump from the page, into your spirit, and grab your attention. God's Word speaks to your spirit and perhaps calls to mind a variety of emotions or thoughts. You may find that it makes a particular point which God seems to be leading you to investigate further. Sometimes this is simply a text which God is bringing to your personal attention, but does not intend you to preach a sermon on it. If it is a text you had not previously noticed, you should perhaps take more time to investigate it. Not every text is the fodder for a sermon; some are just God in His mercy, speaking directly to you, about your need, through His Holy Word.

There are also texts known by preachers as "Great Texts.' The Twenty Third Psalm and John 3:16 are two outstanding texts. One of my favorite texts is John 10:10 "*The thief comes only to steal, to kill and destroy. I am come that they might have life and that more abundantly.*" You might even find a list of great texts if you searched for them on the Internet by the search term "great texts for sermons." If you want to preach on a topic you might do a search for (texts about "insert your topic".) Leave out the brackets in your search term, only enter the search terms.

Another amazing method is to preach through a book or section of the Bible. Many great series have been preached based on The Sermon of the Mount. A favorite section of Scripture which I have preached repeatedly is found in 2

Peter 1:5-11. Navigator publishes scriptures for memorization which are distributed as flash cards. I once preached a series of sermons from a flash card stack on the subject of sin. You can preach series of sermons on broad subjects such as faith, sin, hope, love, salvation, missions, stewardship, habits, family life and personal growth to name only a few.

If you have access to a Naves Topical Bible, you can find groups of texts on hundreds of subjects. Be careful to understand your topic biblically.

4

What Does the Text Say?

The first step is to accurately interpret the text you intend to preach. Interpretation must begin by becoming familiar with the actual words of the text.

You are not ready to begin sermon preparation until you understand, as fully as possible, the meaning of the text. Ask first, what it meant to the writer and those who first heard it. Next, ask how the text has been understood through the history of the church. Finally, ask what the text means to you personally and then, what should this text say to those who hear your sermon on this text.

You are not prepared to answer any of these questions until you grasp the meaning of the text in your own mind. Look away from the printed words and try to recall the full statement of the text. It would be great if you could memorize the text, but many people cannot quickly memorize new verses. You can achieve a fairly complete textual knowledge by reading and re-reading the text. It is also helpful to read the same words from several translations. The goal is to be able to fix the text in your mind.

After the text is fixed in your mind, begin choosing the study aids you will use. This can be the most critical step you make. Unless you understand the text on which you base your sermon, there is a high probability you will not preach a biblically sound message.

A wise man once said: "You can no more teach what you have not learned, than you can return from a place you have not been."

Many ministers report that after studying a text and fixing it into their consciousness the text will unfold in a very natural and comfortable manner for them. At that point, you can begin putting your thoughts about the text onto paper or into your computer. You may also discover this is not a text that you choose to preach. The meaning may point in a direction which you are not prepared to follow at this moment.

Whichever text you decide to use for your sermon, there should be something personal about your choice. The text should speak to you about some element of your life. It may not be about a present problem, but could be about something you dealt with in the past, or anticipate you will be dealing with in the future. It is the personal connection to the text which causes you to be motivated, and motivation produces animation, which produces emotional and intellectual involvement from your hearers.

Whichever text you decide to use for your sermon, there must be something which you believe will meet a need or needs in those who hear it. Unless you achieve this level of connection, you will lose much of your desire to preach the sermon.

Whatever the text has to say or does not say, must guide the elements you incorporate into your sermon. If your sermon reaches beyond your scripture text, your sermon is likely reaching beyond what God intended for you to say on the subject. You are wise to say no more than God says about the thought being explained. Smarter men than me, have looked more foolish than me, when they delved into conjecture and creative explanations of difficult thoughts.

Part Three

STUDY TOOLS

Books In Print

Preachers must choose which study tools to use in developing an understanding of the text and how it applies to the preacher and his hearers.

Preachers use three basic types of tools in sermon preparation. Let's approach each type separately. You will probably settle upon one of these tools as your primary source, so I will separate them into three parts. In my personal study, I use all three. Time and other constraints will limit which tools are available to you.

Most of my life, the only tools available were books in print. When I began preaching, the only study bible in widespread use was The Schofield Study Bible. My parents gave me a clothbound copy of a Schofield Study Bible. For a couple of years it was my only library, I had no other book until I discovered the college library.

We can only use the tools available to us. You can do a lot of good preaching with the 66 books found inside your Bible as your only source. As you acquire other books in your library, it is wise to continue to putting God's Holy Word as your first focus for understanding God's message. He is able to speak very clearly to those who listen.

One of the most remarkable preachers in recent history is the British preacher Major Ian W. Thomas. I have heard him preach on more than a dozen occasions and never ceased to be amazed at his wealth of knowledge and deep understanding of God's Word. His audiences sit in rapt attentions as he preaches. He is quoted as saying, "I only read one book ... the Bible." He was saying that he did not depend on commentaries or the sermons of other preachers to understand or explain the meaning of scripture.

I heard Major Thomas say on several occasions that the Bible interprets itself, with the aid of the Holy Spirit. If you ever read his messages or heard him preach you will be amazed, as audiences have been for more than half a century.

Do not let the smallness of your library become an excuse for poor preparation or sloppy preaching. God will help you develop your skills if you are faithful to Him and follow His leading. He usually does not call the equipped, but He always equips those whom He calls.

For any book or tool to be useful, you must acquire the skills to use it. Memorize the books of the Bible, from beginning to end and in the order of their arrangement. You will need this skill when searching for specific texts.

2

Basic to Ballistic!

Study Bibles lead the field as the most popular learning tool for modern Christians. If I was limited to only two tools, one would be a 'Study Bible' and the other Matthew Henry's commentary on the whole bible. (available as a Kindle book from Amazon.com). There is also a one volume, condensed version of this commentary available as a printed book or ebook. A study bible and some commentary are basic tools in every preacher's tool box.

A basic study bible may only include brief commentary and a concordance for locating specific words. Some extensive study bibles have a page, or pages, describing how to use the tools in the book. Commentary is usually found on the page with the scripture being discussed. Additional tools are located in an Appendix at the rear of the book. The best study bible for you is one you are comfortable using, and is as complete as your budget will allow. When purchasing a study bible, be sure to check out the completeness of the concordance by searching for some familiar passages.

The concordance is a tool used to locate verses of scripture by searching for a single word found in the text of a verse. For example if you search for the word 'love' you should be able to locate 1 Corinthians 13, the famous chapter on love. The concordance is usually located in the back of the book. Do not buy a study bible simply because it is popular as it may not be a good choice for sermon preparation. Several study bibles provide basic background material then become woefully weak in helping interpret specific passages. Many words can be interpreted in a variety of ways. A good study bible will offer alternate readings with a marking immediately next to the word in question.

For many years the Thompson Chain Reference Bible has been a favorite of preachers. It provides suggested outlines and refers the reader to other passages which deal with similar topics. One friend of mine relied completely on this one source for his sermon preparation. No single reference source will answer all your questions, which is why preacher's libraries tend continually to grow.

The NIV Study Bible has been the favorite of laymen and preachers for more than a decade. It has excellent side notes throughout the text and gives a concise, though brief, introduction to each book. The topic or paragraph headings provide a very loose outline of of the subject being covered. I think the NIV Study Bible is also popular because it is a very good devotional bible.

The Ryrie Study Bible was prepared by a renowned scholar, Charles C. Ryrie, who was a renowned and eminent professor at Moody Bible Institute. His is the easiest study bible to use. His comments on verses and passages are priceless. When The Ryrie Study Bible first appeared, I used it for several years, until my copy began to fall apart. When a bible begins to fall apart, you may take that as an opportunity to purchase a version which you do not have in your library.

I no longer go out and buy the 'latest' study bible. You can do so if you are so inclined. Almost every TV evangelist and popular minister produces and sells a study bible named for himself. Be careful about buying a bible that was prepared by authors whose credentials are not available. Cults also publish study bibles. Ask a minister whom you trust about the bible you are considering, and follow his advice. If you are warned away from a version, or system, you probably should heed their advice. If you are still interested in that particular version, simply ask other trusted advisers for their opinion.

There are over 100 versions of study bibles at this time, most are aimed at a particular audience. There are bibles for teens, women, youth, people who are in recovery, those who simply want to understand what the bible says. You certainly do not need every study bible that is in print as many of them simply parrot what was written in other study bibles.

I often use a bible called The Companion Bible. It is very helpful to me. It doesn't provide much commentary, but has an extensive notation system which gives the rudimentary meaning of each important word as it first appears in the book you are reading. The Companion Bible has an extensive appendix to which the reader is referred from within the text. The appendix answers many questions about the meaning of Greek and Hebrew words without requiring the reader to have extensive knowledge of the ancient languages.

None of these books are fully usable until you are familiar with the protocol of how information is presented. Some use different type styles to indicate alternate meanings of certain words. Take time to understand how the book is formatted as this is often the key to understanding or misunderstanding the information provided.

Bible dictionaries are very helpful to explain customs and unusual differences between biblical times and modern usage. Many scholars insist that this should be the second book purchased for your library. These books collect information about persons, places and things into a central location which is indexed by a name or noun. For instance, you might look up "Paul" to find information about the Apostle Paul and find 5 or 10 pages of information outlining the information found about him in scripture as well as extra-biblical information about his life. You would also find information on all others by the same name. The same thing is true if you search for "Jerusalem" or other often mentioned places. Perhaps the most helpful feature will be found in lesser mentioned subjects which are important to your sermon. It is wise to doubt the completeness of your personal knowledge of any subject. The quickest method of supplementing little known facts of bible subjects is the use of a bible dictionary.

Not many people will do what I recently did. I actually read, line by line and page by page, an entire Bible Dictionary. I must admit, I learned things that I had never even casually thought about. Many of them were basic to understanding other important facets of Bible truth. Knowledge is power, but only if you access it.

Anything one can say about the best and latest dictionary would soon be outdated. If you are just beginning to build your library, shop several book stores or catalogs to determine the latest and best on the market. Since these books are updated as new discoveries are uncovered, the newer the better, of they come from a reliable source.

I have made it a hobby to collect Preacher's Annuals. Several denominations and independent publishers publish an annual book which suggests sermons for each service in the year. The details in each annual or manual, as it may be called, vary widely. Most annuals have suggest a sermon for each Sunday and Wednesday service. Some also include children's sermons, funeral sermons and sermons for special occasions. You can glean some very good ideas from these books. Thomas Nelson publishes "Nelson's Annual Preacher's Sourcebook" is one of the best annuals and includes other helpful tools which extend beyond those mentioned above.

You can buy annuals from previous years, both new and used, for much lower prices. If all you want from the book are sermon ideas, it doesn't matter which year it was published. I have annuals in my collection which go back to the early 1920's. In light of a looming economic crisis, I found the annual from 1930 to be especially interesting. You can purchase Minister's Annuals from used book dealers. On line, you can shop Amazon.com, ebay.com or Alibris.com. Alibris operates a network of book dealers and you can often buy books of any genre for below market prices.

Christianbooks.com is one of the best sources for new books. They have an extensive catalog and are a non-denominational company. If you get on their mailing list you will receive catalogs and circulars advertising special sales. It is not uncommon to find book sale bargains from christianbooks.com

Lifeway is best known as the chain store for Christian books. Lifeway.com is the online site for the Lifeway Book Stores. These stores operate under the auspices of the Southern Baptist Convention, but they do not discriminate against other denominations. Lifeway Bookstore also sells materials which you will find to be helpful aids for other aspects of you ministry, such as discipleship materials and graded materials for age groups, or small groups.

Many cities and towns have good Christian bookstores. I like to buy locally when possible. If we don't support our local merchants they can't stay in business. Many Christians would be disadvantaged if they no longer have a local Christian bookstore.

Amazon.com is the largest on line bookseller and should not be overlooked when you are shopping for your print library. They have hundreds of fine commentaries and books on Bible subjects available. I use the Kindle ebook reader from Amazon and have found several useful books in the range from $1 to $10. Some books cost much more than $10, but are consistently less expensive than books on paper. The lower cost of ebooks will quickly cover the cost of the purchase of an eReader device.

Using an eReader makes your printed books more portable, since it is easier to carry one eReader device than to carry a dozen books printed on paper. One eReader, such as Kindle, or nook, or even a smart phone can contain an entire library.

You can download several Bible versions to a Kindle device, Nook, smart phone or other ereader, and have an on-the-go Bible with you at all times.

There is an endless supply of new printed material for preachers. Some of the material is available in both software and printed page format. What you choose to buy is highly personal. Choose the format that works best for your situation. You should also consider the cost as well as future expansion of your study tools.

I enjoy owning the print-on-paper books, but they have a huge disadvantage in that they require a large amount of space to store and are bulky when traveling, which makes them less convenient.

3

Software Solutions

There are a lot of helpful software programs which can be purchased and installed on your PC, MAC, tablet or smartphone. Some of these will be extremely helpful to you. I am not getting into the debate between PC and MAC, as I have never owned a MAC I am confessedly ignorant of any specialized software for the Mac.

Logos Bible Software

The Grandaddy of all Bible software is Logos Bible Software. Logos is available for both Windows and Macintosh computers. It is also available for a wide variety of mobile devices. Since mobile devices are the most rapidly expanding area of technology at this time, we can be sure that this will become a major focus for developers in the future. Logos has a large staff which agressively locates and makes available the newest material as well as some of the older classic works.

Logos makes bible study easier for students at any level of educational advancement. You can begin with a "Starter" package up to a the "Portfolio". Prices vary by the content of the library you choose. They have recently begun producing libraries for specific groups within the Christian community.

There is a special package for Reformed, and Charismatic etc.

Logos Six is the current version of this software at the time of this writing. As newer versions, with improved functionality, become available you are given credit for previous purchases and given an option to upgrade to the newer version. Your entire library will be moved into the latest version when you purchase the upgrade.

Unless you are an extreme bible scholar, you will find limited use for some of the more expensive Logos packages. Inspect the package you expect to buy to determine if you are able to understand and use all the tools it provides. If you do not know Greek and Hebrew, some of the tools would be a waste of your money, but others may help you overcome your deficiency. You can get very near the original meaning of biblical words with the tools available in the starter package. There are some titles which deal specifically with word meanings and do not require actual knowledge of the original languages. Knowledge of original biblical languages is important, but preachers who use their knowledge to impress their audience may be making a mistake. It is usually better to express the meaning of words in terms which listeners can understand and apply to their personal needs.

Logos constantly works to improve their software and include new books. The cost of books added to your library is considerably less than it would be if the books were purchased in print form. As an example: the price of the Portfolio package is $3441.17. If the same books were purchased in new print copies, the cost would be $78,000.00 Many of the books included in the library are no longer available in paper and ink print form. Upcoming new books are offered as pre-pub titles. If a book is purchased 'pre-pub' it usually costs less than the price after publication. Logos uses the pre-pub technique to underwrite the cost of increased expansion, and to determine how popular a proposed publication may be with their customer base.

Logos offers hands-on training seminars for use of their product in various locations throughout the year. These seminars aren't free, but atendees state that the seminars are worth the money.

Wordsearch Preaching Library for Windows

As the title says, this is a preaching library. Other libraries may focus on other aspects of Christian living. Focused bible software is available for teens, women, men and just about any other area of interest you may choose.

Wordsearch software is marketed by Lifeway Christian Resources and makes over 4500 bibles and resources available. My favorite is the Preacher's Outline and Sermon Bible Commentary and Outline Bible. This set is also available in the Lifeway Bookstores in print version. The commentary portion of the set includes recent discoveries as well as classical, the Outline portion provides a broad scope of the material. Inside the commentary, there are numerous segments marked out for "Deeper Thought". Many of these Deeper Thought ideas could become sermons on the same or similar texts. Any area which appears in blue, will hyper link you to the material mentioned in the text by hovering over the blue area.

Starting price for the basic version of Wordsearch is about $305. More extensive versions go up to about $1625. Wordsearch includes a unique audio feature which pronounces over 6,000 difficult to pronounce bible words for the user.

One of my favorite tools in Wordsearch is called Instant Verse Study or IVS. You simply enter the text which you want to study, then click on the IVS icon in the tool bar. The computer will search all the selected books in your library and extract any comments about the text you indicated in the search bar. It takes a few moments for the computer to complete the study. When the search is complete, you can print out the results of the study in your word processor by opening a blank page and clicking paste. You will find it helpful to save the search results in Word before you print it out. You can then edit out extraneous materials before printing. You may choose not to print this material at all and simply read it for background study.

On the Start page, before you enter this software you have three options. You can choose a daily devotional, video tutorials (how to use the software), or Browse Add-0n Books. Like other software developers, Wordsearch is constantly adding new titles and your Internet connection will automatically upload this information as the computer loads the program from your hard drive.

Occasionally Wordsearch upgrades its software. I am running Wordsearch9 and all the new books still work in it. So you aren't pressured to upgrade in order to be able to use new books. Upgrades offer new features that were not imagined or invented at the time of the previous version. Upgrades are always worth the cost and usually take very little time to install. Your old library is automatically moved to the new version of software.

If you use a laptop as well as a PC, you can add the software to multiple computers for no extra charge.

Accordance Bible Software for Macintosh

Accordance Bible Software is available only for Macintosh users. The entry level software is only $179 and prices escalate in keeping with the bundle size increases up to a top price of $1799. I am not a Macintosh owner or user, but this software gets very good reviews from users. Check it out if you are a Macintosh user.

iLumina Gold (for Windows and Macintosh)

This software was published by Tyndale House, one of the oldest and most respected names in Christian publishing. It has digitally scored music and animations. The cost is very reasonable at $89.00, but this software is no longer in production and is only available through re-sellers. No software support is available. You may be interested in it for presentations to youth and children even though use is otherwise limited.

Swordsearcher Bible Software (Windows)

This reasonably priced software for Windows is only $59.95 for the deluxe edition. It comes with a 30-day money back guarantee if you try the free down loadable evaluation version. It has easy and powerful search tools, 18 Bible versions, several dictionaries, commentaries, topical guides, plus maps and illustrations. Preachers on a very limited budget should consider this option.

PC Study Bible Version (Windows)

This is an affordable and powerful Bible study software with five graduations in price and quantity from $37.95 to $449.95. This software is designed for conservative believers and it is packed with commentaries and reference works. This software permits you to use their Biblesoft software to create your own Bible study materials and integrate them into the software.

Ages Software

The Ages Christian Library series is made up of 20 classic bible study books. The entire set can be purchased for $59.95 I own this set and recommend it highly, although it is no longer being supported. You can remove individual books from the collection and use them as standalone books on another PC. This set is heavily weighted toward writings of the Pilgrim Fathers whose work has stood the test of 200 plus years.

Online Options

The absolutely easiest way to get started is to know the text you intend to preach. Let's say that you want to preach on the most widely recognized text in the Bible, which is John 316. Open your browser (google, Bing, Yahoo or whichever) type in the text you are most interested in researching. Then hit enter. You will immediately discover multiple sites that give introductory notes on Bible texts. Open almost any of these sites and scroll down. You will be surprised to find commentaries and in some cases full length sermons on your text. Do not steal another's property, but feel free to "milk the cow" of useful content that fits your sermon plan.

In addition to the above search, there are several websites which offer a wide variety of bible study tools and materials. Internet based software is rapidly gaining popularity among people who prefer to do things online. There is, of course, the hazard of the Internet going down or a site being unavailable when you need it. There are other advantages which outweigh these limitations for many users. Here are a few other starting points for online help.

BibleStudyTools.com

The largest and most popular online resource for Bible study is biblestudytools.com This site has concordances, commentaries, sermons illustrations and many other tools conveniently packaged into one easy to use site. The managers of this site also provide podcast and broadcast capabilities for their users. It is also possible to advertise products within the strict guidlines they have established. I have personally found the online concordances to be the most often used tool. It is extremely easy to look up the location of a word or phrase with this tool. There are also interlinear Greek and Hebrew texts available. You will be very happy with this online resource and the wide variety of helpful features it provides.

eSword

e-Sword - Online Software (Windows) is one of the oldest and best established online software packages on the Internet. This site offers much more than you would expect from a free online software version. You are able to add on other bibles, commentaries and dictionaries. It is easy to use, perhaps the most intuitive Internet software available. There is even a pocket PC version called Pocket e-sword which is available for free. You have nothing to lose, and it is definitely not a waste of time to check this software out.

SermonAudio.com

I mention SermonAudio.com first because it is the preeminent site to listen to sermons online. There are many other such sites including YouTube, but this is the most popular site and you can locate all the others by doing an Internet search for "audio sermons".

Sermon Audio specializes in publishing sermons in the MP3 format. You will either need to purchase an MP3 player or play them through the sound card in your computer. At the time of this writing, there are over 916,000 complete sermons in audio format. They are free to listen to and to download. You are only required to receive a weekly email about updates on the site. A recent development is making some of the sermons available in printable form and some are also available in video.

The sermons on SermonAudio range from sermons being preached currently, to classic recordings of deceased preachers, such as sermons of Charles H. Spurgeon read from Spurgeon's manuscripts by a modern reader. If you are a fan of preaching, you can find sermons by Vance Havner, W. A Criswell, Major Ian W Thomas and countless others.

PreceptAustin.com

PreceptAustin.org is operated as a free to all Bible study site. I mentioned one feature of this site earlier in this book. Precept Austin offers a tutorial on how to do Inductive Bible Study. There is a large online Inductive Bible study ministry operated through this site, which engages groups of people who are not necessarily geographically close to each other, for bible studies If you happen to live in or near Austin, TX you can attend bible studies, with live instructors, from PreceptAustin.

The site opens to about a dozen daily Bible devotions. Beyond the opening page content is an incredible amount of material. The site manager may have some idea how many items are listed here for study, you could never count them. There must be thousands of sermons in print, plus entire commentaries and other study aids as well as a generous number of sermons in audio format. The old standard "Pulpit Commentary" is featured on this site.

If you get stumped on the meaning of a passage, or how to proceed with an outline on a particular text, this is your place to get unstumped. Near the top of the opening page where it simply says choose an option, enter the book in which your text is located. You will be taken immediately to a page with hundreds, perhaps thousands of Bible studies, sermons, lectures, and commentaries dealing with the book you chose. From this point you simply look for the chapter in which your text is found and you will usually find dozens of helps directly related to your text.

I must admit that I have actually lifted entire sermon outlines, and with only slight variations, used them. Years ago Dr J. D. Gray was pastor of New Orleans, LA, First Baptist Church. He was a great preacher with a great comic wit. Folks loved to tease him that he preached other people's sermons. He replied smugly, "When better sermons are written, I'll preach them." Would everyone who refuses to use a better idea please, raise their hand. I thought so.

Searching the Web

There are numerous other sites which offer excellent helps. Some of them charge fees and others operate as free sites. I will not attempt to list every online resource available.

In the Logos Bible Software you can access sermons by preachers who have permitted Logos to post them on their site. You will find this feature at the bottom of the page which shows all results for the search of a text. For example search the text Luke 10:25-37, the parable of the Good Samaritan. At the end of the page it will list sermons on Logos.com There were sermons by four different preachers on that text when I ran my search. It also lists five sermons from SermonCentral.com which are not on the Logos site. The messages in both of these sites are from men of differing denominations and it is interesting to see the different viewpoints taken on the text.

Learning to search the web is a basic skill, but it is easily improved with a little effort. There are several "search engines" which search the entire worldwide web for online specific material in a matter of seconds on popular subjects. I do not endorse one browser above another, but Google, is the most widely used. If you are using a different search engine, you need not change. Each browser performs the same basic function. They search the WorldWideWeb and return the results in a format that let's you make minimal choices. When you see an item of interest you simply click on the heading and the search engine will take you to the site.

Turn on your computer and log on to your search engine. Do a Google search (or Yahoo search etc.) for "sermon texts online" and it will provide you with over 18 million links. Just call me lazy, but I have not yet researched all of the links. The links found on the first page are often the most helpful, but if you don't find what you need on page one, dig deeper, by going to the pages that follow. In examining the links, as always, you will uncover some garbage that is not useful. You also find jewels which are not found anywhere else either on the web or in print.

You can also search for "sermon outlines". Online sermon outlines are often barebone ideas which you need to improve and expand with personal study, research and supplementation. If you find a well written outline, you can "flesh it out" by doing a deeper study of your text.

SermonAudio.com is a tremendous resource for sermon topics, outlines and audio sermons. You can search for sermons by text, topic, speaker, etc. and download them and listen to them on your computer, or MP3 player. I purchased an inexpensive MP3 player to which I download sermons and listen to them while driving, or working in the yard work or other chores which permit me to listen. If you are interrupted you can simply pause the sermon and resume when your situation permits.

No single site is helpful every time you open it. You might be preaching through an Old Testament book and discover that some sites are light on content in some of the Old Testament books. This disparity is why I am listing several sites to consider.

If you search for "sermons on missions" you are returned with over four million links. Some of these links will be useless or repetitions of the same site, that's the nature of the web and online searches. Most links will relate to your search, but you must learn to be selective about which you spend your time reading. There are lots of wild-goose chases available when you do online searches.

If you follow a specific preacher who is well known, there's a good chance you can find his material online. John Piper, John Macarthur and hundreds of others have personal sites which share sermon outlines, and audio sermons. Some even offer video of the sermon that was recorded as it was preached.

You can search for sermons by preachers in your denomination. Search for "methodist sermons" "baptist sermons" or "pentecostal sermons" or whatever your denomination might be, for more selective doctrinal slants on texts. It is good to know how others think and express their ideas. "*Iron sharpens iron.*" Proverbs 27:17. These men are not your enemies, most of them are making a sincere effort to understand and "*rightly divide the word of truth.*"

You can download a bible to your smartphone at Bible.com Other sites offer similar services, but at the time of this writing, Bible.com seems the most popular.

BibleGateway.com has a simple but effective bible study application for the PC and is an excellent place to purchase an audio bible for downloads.

Biblia.com is an online service of Logos Bible Software. It is an excellent site, but the software is much more powerful.

Biblos.com is an extensive Bible study site. This site is also equipped for use on Mobile phones. I am not familiar with the mobile app, but the site for PC's is excellent and very comprehensive.

eBible.org offers a large selection of bibles to download or read online.

studylight.org is an excellent resource for online study. I might have saved the best for last. This site has commentaries, concordances, dictionaries and encyclopedias. That's just the study tools. There are numerous other resources for pastors, study groups, personal devotionals and studies plus historical studies. This definitely is a site you need to check out.

I must offer a caveat to the tools described in this section. <u>Not everything you read on the Internet is true, accurate and reliable</u>. I deliberately left out some sites I found objectionable. Never let the words of any person move your faith in a direction which is not sanctioned, encouraged and taught clearly in God's Word. The same caveat applies to all written materials, but the 'web' is particularly suspect in this regard. An idea can be planted, grow up and bear fruit before its author can be vetted. It is extremely difficult to be certain that quotes from any source are accurately recorded. Be careful! Ask this question: "Does God say that?"

When you borrow material from others, you should make notes on where you found it, who said it, and give appropriate credit to its author. It is also legitimate to change the wording of borrowed ideas. Change the words, the meaning, make it personal. Sometimes a quote is "almost" a good quote ... make it better if you can. Sometimes minor changes create unique ideas.

Think about what you read, or hear in your research as being neatly packaged inside an imaginary box. It is a temptation to simply retell what God gave another servant, in another place, speaking to another group of hearers. Resist that temptation! God is able to give a unique a message to you, for your time and your people. Thinking "outside the box" is essential. You never want to become a Parrot who only repeats what it has heard. God called you to preach His message. He called you because you are uniquely gifted, talented and empowered to express the message He gives to you. You may get assistance from others but like the writer of God's Holy Word you need to learn to trust God so you can honestly declare "*My help comes from the Lord*," Psalm 121:2.

You are going to be happy that you kept reading to this point. I saved the simplest suggestion for last. Using your internet search engine such as Google, Bing, Yahoo etc ... type a Scripture text location into the search box and you will get a boatload of suggestions on that text.

The last paragraph is not a warning to avoid looking to various sources for answers. But don't be a copycat. Someone put it like this: "I milk a lot of cows, but I churn my own butter." That means this: check it all out, but speak the message God gives directly to you. Our God is an awesome God!

Part Four

GATHERING EVIDENCE

1

Take Notes

Studying and reading materials for a sermon can be so
enjoyable that the preacher forgets to take notes. The caution
at this point is: Take notes throughout your process of study,
from beginning to end. Even when you are reading your bible
for daily devotions, you should have a note pad handy
whether physical or digital in form. If a note pad doesn't
work for you, you can also purchase a very small digital
voice recorder and speak your inspirational thoughts into it,
for later replay.

Taking notes to use in building a sermon is similar to what is
done by law officers in criminal investigations, in which
critical evidence is needed in order to get a conviction. The
detective knows there is a crime, but may or may not be sure
exactly how, when or by whom it occurred. The detective
begins gathering bits of evidence. One snippet is found here,
which leads to another snippet in another place.
Following the trail of evidence from one point to another the
culprit is eventually uncovered and the jig is up. If all the
evidence gathered does not result in a firm conclusion of
guilt, it is assumed that the detective missed
something and steps are retraced until the unnoticed evidence
is found. Hopefully, at that point, the new direction will
provide a resolution to the baffling mystery of who done it.

The preacher should never assume that the sermon idea of the text is the one which first seems obvious. Investigate all the textual evidence available and then, only then, determine the direction of your sermon. Like a detective, your goal is to present a message so clearly that it will bring conviction to its hearers.

Detectives are trained to carry a notebook with them when conducting interviews and examining evidence. They write notes to which they later refer and jog their memories about details which might otherwise slip from their memory. I suggest that you do the same thing throughout your day.

Eight sons did milk a bear

Sermons have been found by diligent servants of God in the most obscure and unexpected places.

I heard an amusing story about a preacher who refused to prepare any notes, or even contemplate his text before preaching. He would simply step into the pulpit ... open his bible and blindly place his finger at some point on the page of the open book. Wherever his finger landed he would preach that text.

On one occasion, his finger landed on an obscure text in the book of Hezekiah. He looked, then blinked, then read aloud ... "*Eight sons did milk a bear.*" Suddenly he was desperate. He asked the congregation to pray with him while he sought divine guidance for his sermon.

Suddenly he raised his head with a broad smile and said: "Today's text, "*Eight sons did milk a bear,*'" is one of supreme importance and enlightenment. In this text I see three great biblical doctrines unfolding. The First is the doctrine of Inspiration. These boys had to be inspired in order to attempt milking a bear. Second, is the doctrine of Cooperation. Each son must do his part in order to successfully and completely milk the bear. Thirdly is the grand doctrine of Progressive Inspiration, cCause we all know nowadays that bear's milk aint no good noway."

I have never been able to convince myself that I was capable of such inspired deliverance, so I prepare as diligently as I can.

Get It On Paper

The first step in functional organization is to put it on paper or some digital format. You may choose to underline or mark passages you read and refer back later, but that has always proved to be hit and miss for some preachers. If you are using computer software, you can usually click and paste to a word document. Some bible study software contains a simple word processor to use for note taking. You may find that it is more convenient to keep all your notes in a single location.

My practice is to gather all my notes to a single location. My first notes usually go onto a note pad or slip of paper on my desk, or in my Bible. As my sermon outline begins to take shape, I go to the bottom of the notes and begin my outline at that point. As I use items from my notes, or discard ideas, I delete them. At the end of fleshing-out my outline I usually am able to discard the rest of my notes and am left with only the document which becomes my sermon outline. Many of the study aids you use will indicate other verses of scripture which add substance and verify that your sermon is not a verse which has no background authority.

Make lists of these scriptures and indicate in your notes the principal point which they support. You will later choose to read some of these verses as part of your sermon. One of the best features of The Preacher's Outline and Sermon Commentary, is that supporting verses are listed within the commentary. Another method is to do a backward search in a Nave's Topical Bible by finding your text, then noticing the subject categories in which it is placed.

However you choose to take notes, it is important to be able to refer back to your scribbles. You might even choose to put your notes into a portable device that you carry with you. This lets you find time to revisit them during down times of an active schedule.

When using WordSearch, you can perform a feature called Instant Verse Study or "IVS". In the search box, enter the location of the text you are studying, then click on the Instant Verse Study Icon at the top of the page. In a short period of time the program will search all the books you specify and collect the information into a printable form. You can open your word processor to a blank document, click "paste", and all the material collected by the program will populate the screen. Not all the information garnered will be useful. Simply go through the material and delete any valueless type before you print it. Much of the content will simply tell you that nothing was found in a source you had chosen to search.

Going back to the illustration of a detective seeking evidence about the perpetrator of a crime; most detectives begin to select suspects prior to determining the guilt of a single party. If your background study of a text is thorough and conclusive you will probably see the form of a sermon begin to take shape. It is easier to reach a destination which is clearly identified and marked in your mind.

Jot down in short form, the idea or ideas you think will become the final sermon, delete and add as needed. Once the main point is clarified, the route to it is easily mapped.

It is where it is

You are unlikely to find all the material for your sermon in one location although some sermons seem to simply tumble right out of the verses of your text. It is not unusual for full sermons to be completed without studying any material other than your bible. It would be wonderful if all preaching could be done in that manner. Most often, we search multiple sources. When you switch from a commentary to a bible dictionary or an audio sermon it is easy to lose a train of thought in the process. It is helpful to note the exact location in which you found a morsel of information, although there are times we need only to jot down a reminder of the thought. To note the location of useful ideas from an audio sermon ... take note of the play-time, or how long the sermon has been playing. You can quickly scroll back to a location in an audio sermon in this manner.

While audio sermons are enjoyable and informative, one should take notes during the process of listening. Simply pause your audio player and make a note. The next word spoken often forces the information or idea you wanted, right out of your mind. If a notepad isn't handy, you can voice record a thought in the voice recorder of your cell phone or digital recorder.

Finding the right word or thought is too difficult to risk losing it by negligence. You could literally spend hours each week trying to relocate what you previously located. We must not fail to collect the evidence we find.

In big city police forces, one detective must take such accurate notes that another detective can take over his investigation without losing a beat. It is unlikely someone else will ever need to use your sermon notes, but you may want to use them again at a much later time. Unless you do a good job of collecting and organizing your notes they will be useless after some period of time has elapsed.

Examine every idea you have, which may find its way into a sermon. God cautioned His prophet in these words: "*My thoughts are not your thoughts.*" Isaiah 55:8. Our thought may sound good to us, but may not survive the microscope of God's Word. Don't be discouraged to learn that your thoughts went astray ... be thankful that God in His mercy brought you back into correct thinking.

Resist the reflexive temptation to organize your sermon before you have completed background study. You don't want to spend the day polishing an apple, imaginatively savoring its juices, then to discover it is made of wax. Don't hastily put your thoughts into organized form before you know for certain you have discovered what God wants to say to you and your listeners.

One day in a college bible class I had a moment of clarity. My teacher had just finished an elegant explanation of a difficult biblical concept which left the entire class in awe. He then looked at me and said, "Mr Taylor, if you can memorize what I've just said, you will have it all in a nutshell." I had never thought of my skull as a nutshell, but I fully understood his point.

Unless you take good notes as you study; when you realize you cannot locate an important item you will realize ... 'you put it all in a nutshell.'

3

Organize It

Organize your notes into a planned presentation. Let's return to the detective analogy. A detective turns his notes over to a prosecuting attorney who presents the case in court. Your task is as crucial as that of an attorney. Lives hang in the balance, eternity looms, God is listening, do your best work at this stage of preparation. Be inventive, be imaginative, but be sound in your doctrine.

The text often dictates the order in which truth is presented. This is especially true in sermons based on stories or parables. God has powerful ways to communicate His ideas. Think long and hard before you attempt to revise the order of His thoughts.

As you organize, choose points at which you need to inject humor, illustrations, changes of pace or style, emotional triggers, stories, poetry or simple voice modulation. You can invent a "secret" code to note the points where you want to inject changes of manner or style. If these seem to be trivial suggestions you must remember that a good idea never achieves its full value unless it is remembered by the hearer. Most scholars postulate that this is why Jesus used abundant parables in His preaching.

Reduce ideas into bite sized portions

A speech professor told our class: "It isn't enough to kill a deer; it needs to be dressed." He referred to skinning, butchering and cutting the carcass into usable portions of food. When we prepare to preach we cannot chew, swallow or digest the message for our congregation, but we can present the truth in consumable portions, if not in an appetizing manner. Many sermons can be greatly improved by simply shortening them. Do not attempt to give your audience larger bites than they can chew and swallow.

When you preach, keep your audience in mind. Ask yourself how the listener will hear and respond to the methods you choose. In Collossians 4:6, Paul indicates that there is a proper way to share any truth with others. *"Let your speech always be with grace, seasoned with salt, that you may know how you ought to answer each one."* Theaters thrive on shock values, shock is a Hollywood gimmick, but we are not entertainers who present the truth by attempting to thrill or frighten our audience. The fear of God comes upon those whom He chooses.

Illustrate the meaning

They say a picture is worth a thousand words. A sketch artist must have fostered that idea. It is impossible to quote a picture. It is possible to share an idea. An idea is worth more than a thousand pictures. It is difficult to find pictures which convey an exact message. Jesus told stories and quoted the thoughts and ideas of others. In so doing, He planted ideas into the minds of His hearers. The common people heard Him gladly, while religious leaders scoffed at every word and miraculous sign. If people aren't listening, you might as well be silent.

I am not against the use of pictures, but in many settings it is not feasible to use them. Flannel graphs and 'story boards' are still being used very effectively. Chalk artists have also fascinated and informed congregations in a powerful manner. Today with the advent of computers, some are placing helpful pictures on large screens to help their audience"see" an idea.

Illustrations demonstrate concepts, but are also used to hold the attention of listeners. Both are valid uses of illustrations. Words rightly used ignite flames within the minds and spirits of hearers. Choose powerful illustrations.

The most common illustrations and attention-getting devices are quotes, poems, stories, statistics, humor, varied rates of speech, changes in volume or intensity, statistics and maintaining eye contact

Sermon illustrations are easily found on the Internet. If you want a poem, search for poems on the main theme of your message. ("poems on faith") in google or another search engine will produce pages of sources. The same thing is true of humor. ("jokes on lying") or most other subjects will quickly appear. Both Logos and WordSearch utilize a book with 15,000 sermon illustrations. The sermon illustrations are listed under topical names and you will learn quickly how to best search these topics to satisfy your needs.

One of the most comprehensive locations for illustrations on the Internet is: http://www.sermonillustrations.com I use this

resource often and highly commend it for your
consideration.

Reduce the Size

You didn't do it intentionally, but in your zest to cover it all,
you most likely put things into your organized material which
are only marginally related to the finished structure you are
attempting to build.

Examine each small segment and sentence. Ask yourself if
these words contribute to understanding or acceptance of the
message from God's Word. Do they advance the objective of
making clear the meaning of your text? Does this thought or
sentence seem out of place? Will they motivate the hearer to
act on God's message to them?

Do the same thing with illustrations, poems, jokes and other
forms of material. The "stuff" you remove can be saved for
use in other messages, but not everything on a subject can be
made to fit into a clearly focused sermon.

The mind will no longer absorb when the behind will no
longer endure! At some point a sermon must conclude. At a
rescue mission, where I preached, the pulpit had a slogan
plastered to its face. "If after 30 minutes you haven't struck
oil ... stop boring." One of the most difficult duties of a gifted
preacher is to limit his remarks to a certain time period,
without limiting the congregations opportunity to know the
truth.

Take notice of how full your outline or manuscript is and
then note how long it takes you to deliver it. By this simple

trial and error practice, most preachers are able to grip their congregation without a gripe. The more years you preach to the same congregation, the more urgent it is to pace yourself to an acceptable time period for your sermons. Set the length of time you preach by the audience you are addressing. Children have shorter attention spans than adults. But if your message is entertaining you can flip the diagram.

In my preaching, I use an outline of no more than a single page in Wednesday night prayer services. Notes for my Sunday sermon are limited to two pages. It isn't perfect, because the man who preaches from these notes is far from perfect ... but it helps me keep it between the ditches. Most of the time I manage to quit preaching before they quit listening. As my good friend Dizzy Dean use to say: "If you done it, it ain't bragging."

4

Trim the Fat

This is the final step before preaching your sermon. Hopefully you have gathered great material that could grip an audience for ten hours. We both know that they will not stay that long. So it is time to disgorge any 'stuff' that does not belong in the pulpit.

It is time to begin putting the finishing touches on your masterpiece. Your prime objective should be that your message is clear and understandable. Excess words, sentences and paragraphs which do not speak directly about the subject of your message need to be deleted. Sermons do not need 'filler material' to make them a certain length. The difficult task for most preachers is not being able to preach long enough, but being able to trim their messages so they say all they need to say, and no more.

Making your message clear and understandable is your first objective. Have you ever had a problem with some utility service, only to call the service department and be placed on a call with a person who does not speak your language. The accent of people who came to America from a country in which they speak a different language is very difficult to understand when we are face to face, the difficulty multiplies when speaking on the telephone. Preachers should be concerned about how they speak. Your words need to be understandable. It is a good practice to record your sermons and listen critically to what you say, how you say it and notice any abnormalities in your speech which you can correct.

One method of making your central point understood and clearly defined is to create a succinct sentence. At various stages in your sermon you can ask the congregation to repeat aloud the keynote sentence. The sentence can be a verse of scripture such as "*It is not God's will that any should perish, but that all should come to repentance.*" Asking your congregation to repeat this sentence at several points in your sermon delivery will fix the scripture in their minds and tie your message together ... assuming that you are preaching the central meaning of your text. You could also use a sentence like this: "God wants all believers to be witnesses for Jesus." This would go well with a sermon on the Great Commission or any other message on evangelism.

I have never pre-recorded my sermon and listened to it before actually preaching, but I've heard that some preachers use this practice as a learning tool. As you listen to recordings of your messages you should ask a few basic questions.

Are you making any annoying vocal pauses. A vocal pause can be as simple as 'uhh', or can be phrases like youth use ...'you know' or 'like'. A vocal pause is any sound inserted into a spot which would otherwise contain only silence. Vocal pauses irritate some people so badly that they refuse to listen to that person speak. An appropriate vocal pause is to simply remain silent for a short moment. Silence can be a tremendous attention device.

Are there words you do not pronounce clearly? In college speech classes we were sent to the "Speech Lab" once a week. We would listen to a recorded list of vocabulary words and repeat and record them alongside those on the recording. We tried to say the word exactly as on the recording. After we had gone through the entire list, we would listen to a tape which played the correct pronunciation followed immediately by our effort. One word I remember well was "athlete." When I pronounced it I added a letter to the word and pronounced it "ath-a-lete", which is incorrect. I have noticed, that the commentators on ESPN make the same error. If you have very bad speech habits, you should consider enrolling in a corrective course at a nearby community college to attempt to correct them.

Scripture readings are especially difficult. Here's a suggestion that may help you improve in this area. Acquire a recording of your text which is read by a good reader and read aloud along with the recording. You will soon discover your weakest points and be able to correct them. You can find scripture recordings on SermonAudio.com.

Pay close attention to descriptive terms you use. Are you using words with which your audience is familiar? Do they use the words, in the same manner, with the same meaning they assign to them?

Some people have speech abnormalities which are not correctable. I once knew a preacher who had suffered from lockjaw as a young man. God called him to preach and he began preaching. It was extremely difficult to understand some of his words, since he could not close his jaw. If you listened intently, after a few minutes you began to ignore his impediment and could understand what he was saying very easily. He did not let his disability prevent him from following God. If God could only use perfect men, none of us would be preachers.

Avoid Repetition. Avoid Repetition! And don't repeat yourself!

A preacher is often accused of repeating himself. This is seldom done intentionally. There are many ways in which this flaw can occur, but there are two ways to note frequent offenders.

Once you have completed a point. Do not repeat it unless you so plan to emphasize a recurrent theme. Many people repeat in one concise statement the main points, but if you do, do not expound them again.

Don't preach the same sermon in close vicinity to the last time you preached it. Keep a record of (1) texts preached (2) Subjects preached. Do not repeat yourself with such regularity that your audience begins to notice. it. You may have a favorite singer, but if you could only listen to a limited number of that singer's songs, you might become bored with listening to her sing.

Predictability is not a problem for any pastor during his first few months in a new pulpit. There is an old joke about preachers having three points and a poem. Somewhere along the way, stereotypes of preachers and preaching began to develop. If you will vary your style, subject and type of background material with regularity, you can avoid the boredom of predictability. Listen to several preachers on the same text at SermonAudio.com. You will notice that there are many ways to preach the same truth from the same text.

Pattern your sermon plea after one which is very different from the others, but is thoroughly sound doctrinally. Avoid being predictable.

Inject Moments of Interest

Choose a snappy sermon title. Try not to be completely obscure, but the title is more of an attention getting device. The title is a phrase which directs and limits your message. The catchy title can often come from a feature in the scripture. I once preached a sermon about the incident where Samson killed a thousand men with the jawbone of an ass. I called the sermon "Jawbone Hill." There is some precedent since the heap was called by that name. It made an interesting point out of a fact that would otherwise find no place in the sermon.

Decide which illustration best explains your subject and place it near the beginning of your message. Decide which illustration best motivates listeners to surrender to the call of God in your sermon and place that illustration at or near the end of your message. Other illustrative material should be placed directly by the points which the illustration best suits.

When you move from one theme to another it is a good practice to inject humor as you introduce the next point. Unless we flag the transition in some manner, the audience will often drift out of the flow of thought.

We do not preach to please men, but we should not preach to deliberately antagonize them. Jesus often seems to be an antagonist. However, if you closely inspect his responses you will find that the major element taught a truth so timeless that it applied to His accusers and still reproaches men today. We often try to be timely when we should be trying to be timeless. Our message should ring the same bell after much time has passed. Solid truth should not have to apologize for being boring. Think of ways that God can use your unique personality to minister His word through you. Preachers are not boring because they plan to be boring, they are boring because they didn't plan to avoid boredom.

—

Part Five

THE APPEAL

1

Plan Your Appeal

No moment of a sermon is more important than the appeal. A study of sermon appeals could become a book itself. I suggest that you read sermons by great preachers and you will find vast differences in their approaches.

The appeal may be the moment when preachers should be most spontaneous. Even if you have a well planned appeal, be willing to quickly abort it in favor of leadership from the Holy Spirit. The invitation is the explicit property of the Holy Spirit. Jesus promised that "*He will convict the world of sin, and of righteousness, and of judgment to come.*" Those are the steps which a lost sinner must take in order to surrender control of his life to the Lord Jesus Christ.

An appeal should, be distinct and clear.
An appeal should, be solidly based on scriptural mandates.
An appeal should, be based on establishing proper relationships with Christ.
An appeal should mention the danger of disobeying God's call.

An appeal should not indicate that a purely emotional, or intellectual decision is acceptable to God. An appeal should not cheapen grace. Dietrich Bonhoeffer described a faulty description of grace with his term "cheap grace."

"Cheap grace is the grace we bestow on ourselves.
Cheap grace is the preaching of forgiveness without requiring repentance,
baptism without church discipline,
communion without confession ...
Cheap grace is grace without discipleship,
grace without the cross,
grace without Jesus Christ living and incarnate." --Dietrich Bonhoeffer *"The Cost of Discipleship"*

2

Plan to Stand Your Ground

Ephesians 6 tells us to *"put on the whole armor of God."*
After we have armed ourselves with those powerful spiritual
weapons, the final command is *"to stand."* There will be
times when men oppose you. The opposition of men is the
least of your concerns. We are in a battle with the forces of
evil. Satan will attack you far more often than men. He is
opposed to the gospel, which makes every minister of God a
target of his attacks. You are on the firing line with God's
troops. Never retreat without clear orders from the Lord.
Trust his grace to sustain you whether the attacks are
physical, social, financial or spiritual. The Lord Jesus has
promised to always be with you, *"even unto the end of the
age."*

Romans 8:31 reminds us *"If God be for us who can be
against us."* Preaching, even great preaching, is not intended
for the pleasure of men, but it must always please God. Those
who seek the approval of men upon their message, do so at
the peril of preaching without the anointing of God. God is
always pleased when we obey Him, and always displeased
when we refuse to obey Him.

There will be times when men will love you, but despise your
message. Other men may dislike you personally, but love
your message. Neither of these circumstances should

encourage or discourage God's man. We preach by a mandate from God. By our obedience to God's mandate men are saved, lives are transformed, churches are built and grow, homes become havens of rest, Heaven gains new citizens and the kingdom of God is expanded throughout the world.

Preaching is how we deliver ourselves from the burden of our calling. Our calling is the same as the prophet Ezekiel, the Old Testament prophet. When God called Ezekiel he said *"Son of man, I have made you a watchman for the house of Israel."* We preach to lost sinners as well as to men made righteous by the blood of Jesus. We call each of them to repentance, to enduring faith in Jesus and to faithful living for the Lord God. *"Nevertheless if you warn the righteous man that the righteous should not sin, and he does not sin, he shall surely live because he took warning; also you will have delivered your soul."* Go and do thou likewise.

Conclusion

You may recall what I said in the beginning: this is only a basic lesson in sermon preparation. Your first attempts to use these methods may be clumsy or amazingly brilliant. No matter which outcome you achieve, one sermon does not complete an entire ministry of preaching. If at first you don't succeed, try, try again. If children stopped trying to walk when they had fallen a few times, they would miss the joy, not only of walking, but of running and jumping as well. You will certainly stumble and fall. Hopefully you will rise and try again and again. If God has called you to preach, He will help you to preach. God seldom calls men who are already equipped to preach. But He faithfully equips those whom He has called. I pray He will use these elementary ideas to speed you on your way.

Rev. Wharton, a Presbyterian pastor who labored more than 50 years in my little hometown of Long Beach, MS was an inspiration to my life as well as every boy in town. He had a rhyme that he taught us kids. It went like this,

"Good better best,
Never let it rest,
until your good is better,
and your better is your best."

I have guided my life by that motto. It has proven especially appropriate to the labor of learning to preach. Never quit growing. I'm told that when we quit growing, we start dying.

As your skills improve and you realize you have not peaked in your abilities, you should seek out more advanced studies to help you move forward. There are many faithful, godly men whom God has moved to write on the subject of preaching. Find their works and absorb the help they can give you. Each topic I touched is only the opening to a gold-mine of truth and training which can be realized through further studies. If you have the opportunity to get formal education in either a college or seminary, choose the school carefully, but seize the chance to learn more fully the things I could only drop hints about in this brief effort.

Here is one last idea which will help you continue to grow as a preacher. Growing can be compared to using a ladder. What is above your reach without help, can probably be reached with the help of a ladder. Use the help you find in this book as the first rung on a ladder to preaching excellence. As soon as you are comfortable with these tools and techniques you need to stretch your imagination and further elevate your abilities. Take advantage of every opportunity you can find to learn how to improve your preaching skills.

One simple step you can take is to read the sermons of great preachers and notice how they connect their thoughts. You might want to check out the sermons of Dr. D. Martyn Lloyd-Jones who has been called the prince of modern preachers. He was a Baptist preacher in London. Another excellent preacher was Dr. James Montgomery Boice. Dr. Boice was pastor of Third Presbyterian Church in Philadelphia, PA. Both men were excellent scholars. They fully believed in the authority of the Scripture and took great pain to make their message understandable to all who listened. Although these men are now deceased, their style and subject matter may never become outdated. Both were excellent scholars as well as successful pastors. Each served lengthy pastorates, which demands strenuous effort from the preacher to remain relevant and fresh. There are other good preachers, of course, these are simply two who have been helpful to me. The printed works of each of these men is readily available in many book stores and some of their work is already online. These are not the only preachers I have leaned upon, but you will find your own favorites. May God bless you as you do.

I have already begun to pray for those who will read these words. May God bless you.

Made in the USA
Monee, IL
23 April 2023

32286957R10059